Every Christian Is an Evangelist

Every Christian Is an Evangelist

Biblical Motivations for Sharing the Gospel

Brian G. Najapfour

Foreword by Joel R. Beeke

PAIDEIA PRESS

Every Christian Is an Evangelist
© 2024 by Brian G. Najapfour

All rights reserved. Except for brief quotations in critical publications or reviews, no part of this book may be reproduced in any manner without prior written permission from the publisher.

Paideia Press
3248 Twenty First St., Jordan Station,
Ontario, Canada L0R 1S0
www.paideiapress.ca

Unless otherwise indicated, Scripture quotations are from the New King James Version®. Copyright © 1982 by Thomas Nelson. Used by permission. All rights reserved.

Book Design by Amy Zevenbergen
ISBN 978-0-88815-349-4

RECOMMENDATIONS

Few could read this book without being simultaneously convicted and encouraged in our evangelistic task. With gospel-fueled enthusiasm, Dr. Najapfour urges us to abandon our excuses and embrace the joy and privilege of speaking about the Christ who saved us.
—Dr. Reuben Bredenhof, Professor of Ministry and Mission, Canadian Reformed Theological Seminary

Reading this book will help you become a more faithful witness of Christ. After defining the terms, Dr. Najapfour first persuasively encourages us to share the gospel with unbelievers. Then he pastorally removes our excesses for not evangelizing more faithfully. Our greatest hindrance is often personal motivation. This book, which is thoroughly Reformed, will help resolve that problem.
—Dr. Brian A. DeVries, Principal of Mukhanyo Theological College, South Africa

What makes Dr. Najapfour's loving and compelling exhortation to evangelize so credible is that he consistently practices what he preaches! He irrefutably argues from Scripture that every Christian is called to communicate Christ's gospel to his or her perishing neighbor. May God use this booklet to awaken us to engage prayerfully, willingly, and consistently in our much-neglected calling.
—Rev. Bartel Elshout, pastor of Kalamazoo Reformed Church, Michigan

Simple yet profound, this book is indeed evangelism for everyone. Every believer should always take time to rehearse the simplicity and profundity of the gospel. One way is by letting the heart-cry of this book permeate the totality of our redeemed humanity to be enthused and satisfied as gospel-mouthpieces. Reading brings tons of encouragement and warning.
—Rev. Leonardo F. Galanza Jr., President of the Center for Biblical Studies, the Philippines

Dr. Najapfour not only clarifies the terms *evangelism* and *gospel* but also offers biblical motivations why Christian should engage in evangelism, and pastorally counsels those who avoid this practice. Warmly recommended.
—Dr. Adriaan C. Neele, President of Puritan Reformed Theological Seminary, Michigan

Beware to read this book, as it will deprive you of any excuse to be a witnessing Christian. But if you want to be one, this book will certainly inspire you.
—Dr. Herman Selderhuis, Theological University of Apeldoorn, the Netherlands

All Christians need regular exhortations to bear witness to the truth. This book is a quickening to the slow to speak, an encouragement to the shy, an instruction to the novice, and a God-centered motivator to every believer. Take and read!
—Dr. Geoffrey Thomas, author of *In the Shadow of the Rock*

The gospel of Jesus Christ is the greatest news in history. Yet, for many of us who are Christians, we often struggle with telling others about Christ and the salvation He gives. Sadly, the practice of personal evangelism is sometimes understood today as entirely the duty of "professional" Christians—pastors, elders, seminary professors, missionaries, evangelists, and the like. But as Dr. Najapfour contends, sharing the gospel is an essential part of the Christian life and therefore the responsibility of every Christian. With five convincing arguments explaining why all Christians must evangelize—or "gospelize" as Najapfour puts it—and five convicting responses to objections some of us raise for avoiding evangelism, *Every Christian Is an Evangelist* is a challenging reminder of the sacred calling we all share as followers of Christ to point others to Him.
—Dr. John W. Tweeddale, Vice President of Academics and Professor of Theology, Reformation Bible College, Florida

DEDICATED TO
Rev. Gilbert (Bong) Lugtu
and
Rev. Wilfredo (Willy) Cruz Jr.
*my two spiritual fathers who
evangelized and discipled me.*

TABLE OF CONTENTS

Foreword... xi
Preface.. xv

1. Introduction.................................... 1
What Is Evangelism?
What Is the Gospel?

2. Five Reasons Why All Christians Must Evangelize.................................... 9
Evangelism Is a Way of Life
Evangelism Is Part of Our Identity in Christ
Evangelism Arises from Our Love for Unbelievers
Evangelism Originates in the Very Nature of God
Evangelism is a Command as Set Forth in the Great Commission

3. Five Excuses Some Christians Use for Not Evangelizing.................................. 23
I Am Not Worthy; Who Am I?
I Do Not Know What to Say
They Will Not Believe Me
I Am Not Eloquent
I Do Not Want to Do It; Please Send Someone Else

4. Conclusion 41
    Challenge to Unbelievers
    Challenge to Believers

Appendix 1: Discussion Questions.................. 57
Appendix 2: Recommended Books on Evangelism..... 65
Appendix 3: A Gospel Tract 67

FOREWORD

Everyone has a message of hope—a gospel (or "evangel")—for the world. For some, that message of hope is the false evangel of salvation through scientific, medical, or technological innovation; for others, it is the evangel of economic or racial emancipation as salvation; for still others, it is the evangel of false hope from false religion. Not only is every follower of Jesus Christ an evangelist, but in a sense, everyone—believer and unbeliever alike—is an evangelist. *You*, too, are an evangelist, dear reader.

Our question, then, must be this: Do you have the right gospel? What gospel are you proclaiming to believe through your life and actions? Only the gospel of Jesus Christ is the truth and offers escape from the curse of sin and its eternal punishment. This true gospel is synonymous with Jesus Christ in His person (as truly God and truly man) and His work (in His active and passive obedience).

In motivating God's people to share the only message of hope for mankind, my friend Dr. Brian Najapfour, who is an alumnus of our seminary and a fellow colleague in the ministry in our denomination, begins by defining evangelism and the gospel. He describes how authentic evangelism is the act of faithfully proclaiming the gospel, God's message of salvation through Jesus Christ. We complicate evangelism because we complicate the gospel, Dr. Najapfour says. We try to soften the offense of the gospel, losing the beauty and simplicity of the message in the process. He then responds to the myriad excuses we often find for avoiding evangelism—"alibis," as he calls them—and encourages believers to instead pray and look for opportunities to call others to faith and repentance in Christ out of love for both God and our neighbor.

This booklet is thoroughly Reformed. As Dr. Najapfour demonstrates, the Reformed emphasis on the sovereignty of God in salvation helps rather than hinders evangelism. Indeed, the Reformed movement put modern missions on the map in certain areas where the Reformed found access to do so (recall that John Calvin sent missionaries to Brazil). Furthermore, as our spiritual forefathers articulated in our Reformed confessions, believers participate in Christ's threefold office as prophets, priests, and kings. It is only in the self-awareness of our identity as prophets, or those who proclaim the message of God, that evangelism becomes a lifestyle—not simply something we *do*, but the overflow of who we *are*, for identity determines action. As prophets, however, we must expect rejection, persecution, opposition, and weakness, but it is in that very weakness that we draw strength from Christ (2 Cor. 12:10).

As Dr. Najapfour demonstrates, evangelism is a way of life for the Christian; it is exciting; and it is an activity commanded by God. Yet he is careful to ground motivation for evangelism in the promises of God, the love of God, and gratitude toward God—instead of from a spirit of guilt or duty. Let us meditate often on the cross of Christ and the fires of hell, for such reflection can stir our hearts, by God's grace, with love for the lost. Let us evangelize the lost because we love them. Above all, we reflect God—the great Evangelist—when we share the gospel with others.

After reading this manual, I pray with my dear brother that the next time you interact with unbelieving neighbors—whether in your community, at the barbershop, at a restaurant, or on an airplane—you will be able to share the gospel with them. May the Lord richly bless you with this little yet important book.

Joel R. Beeke
Puritan Reformed Theological Seminary, Chancellor
Grand Rapids, Michigan

PREFACE

In August 2013, I delivered a speech on evangelism at the Puritan Reformed Conference in Michigan. That speech, entitled "Living Evangelistically: Biblical Motivation for Proclaiming the Gospel," was eventually published as chapter seven in *The Beauty and Glory of Christian Living* (2014). The book you are reading is an expanded version of that chapter.

I could not have finished this work without my dear wife Sarah, who helped me improve the manuscript. Thank you for your constant support and encouragement.

I also wish to thank Gina Bessetti-Reyes for editing this book. Likewise, I am grateful to August Merz for his proofreading help, to Linda den Hollander for her neat typesetting, and to Amy Zevenbergen for the creative cover design.

A special word of gratitude also goes to John Hultink and Steven Martins of Paideia Press for publishing this work.

Finally, I thank and praise Christ Jesus for saving

me and giving me the privilege to share His gospel with others.

> *I thank Christ Jesus our Lord who has enabled me,*
> *because He counted me faithful,*
> *putting me into the ministry.*
> *Now to the King eternal, immortal, invisible,*
> *to God who alone is wise,*
> *be honor and glory forever and ever.*
> *Amen* (1 Tim. 1:12, 17).

CHAPTER ONE

Introduction

In this book, I will present five reasons why *all* Christians must engage in evangelistic work. Then I will respond to five excuses that some Christians use to avoid the work of evangelism. I want to begin, however, by clarifying the meaning of two important terms: *evangelism* and *gospel*.

What Is Evangelism?
The English term *evangelism* comes from the Greek word *euangelion*, meaning "evangel" or "gospel." So, to evangelize (evangel) is simply to gospelize (gospel), or to proclaim the gospel of the Lord Jesus Christ. For this reason, broadly speaking, an "evangelist" or "gospelist" is any Christian who faithfully shares God's message of salvation through Christ with others. All of us, then, who are in Christ and are faithfully sharing the biblical gospel are evangelists.

However, in the stricter sense, an evangelist is a divinely gifted person whose primary calling is to proclaim the Good News. In the Bible, the word *evangelist* only appears three times. It first appears in Acts

21:8: "On the next day we who were Paul's companions departed and came to Caesarea, and entered the house of Philip the evangelist, who was one of the seven, and stayed with him."[1] Here, Philip, one of the seven deacons of the church in Jerusalem (Acts 6:5), is described as "Philip the evangelist," because he has been specifically tasked by God to proclaim the gospel (8:40)[2], although essentially (as we will see later) every true Christian is called to do the same task. Remember, all Christians are "ambassadors for Christ," having been given by God "the ministry of reconciliation" (2 Cor. 5:18–20). This ministry involves the proclamation of "the word of reconciliation," which is basically the gospel (v. 19). As ambassadors for Christ, all Christians have a divine mandate to call the unbelievers on God's behalf to be reconciled to Him through Christ, which is another way of saying: Believe in the Lord Jesus Christ, and you will be saved (Rom. 5:10).

Nonetheless, much like a missionary, a person who has been specially called by God to be an evangelist does not typically stay in one place, but travels from one place to another to keep reaching out to the

---

[1]. The other two verses in which the term *evangelist* appears are Ephesians 4:11 and 2 Timothy 4:5. Unless noted otherwise, all scriptural quotations are taken from the New King James Version (NKJV).

[2]. That verse reads: "But Philip was found at Azotus. And passing through, he preached in all the cities till he came to Caesarea." In the original, the designation "he preached" is one word: *euēngelizeto*, which literally means "he was proclaiming the gospel."

spiritually lost with the Good News. The itinerant evangelist Billy Graham (1918–2018) was a modern example of this. In this study, however, I will use the term *evangelism* in its broader sense, as it refers to the glorious work of *every* Christian to share the gospel with others. Thus, I entitled my book *Every Christian Is an Evangelist: Biblical Motivations for Sharing the Gospel with Others*. And as the subtitle indicates, my goal in this study is to encourage and challenge *all* Christians to be actively sharing the gospel, "for it is the power of God to salvation for everyone who believes" (Rom. 1:16).

In his sermon on Romans 1:14, which he titled "Every Christian a Debtor to the Pagan," the Presbyterian theologian William G. T. Shedd (1820–1894) shared my main thesis when he said, "Every individual member of the Christian Church *owes* the gospel to mankind. Each and every disciple of Christ must say with St. Paul: 'I am debtor both to the Greek and the Barbarians, both to the wise and the unwise.'"[3] Shedd argued how "St. Paul was not under any such special and peculiar indebtedness, in this particular, as to make his position different from yours and mine.... All Christians stand upon the same position, in regard to the work of evangelizing the world. They are all of them debtors."[4]

---

3. William G. T. Shedd, "Every Christian a Debtor to the Pagan," in *Sermons to the Spiritual Man* (New York: Charles Scribner's Sons, 1884), 386.

4. Shedd, "Every Christian a Debtor to the Pagan," 385–86.

We must not think that the gospel is only for unbelievers, though, because those of us who are in Christ still need it, too! The gospel is for all sinners, saved or unsaved. On occasion, I've heard Christians say something like, "I'm already saved and no longer need to hear the gospel." This sort of thinking is unscriptural because we never stop needing to hear the gospel. In Philippians 1:27, Paul exhorts the Philippian believers to conduct themselves according to the gospel: "Only let your conduct [or, manner of life] be worthy of the gospel of Christ." Put differently, as believers we should consistently live in a way that's worthy of the gospel and visibly demonstrates our glorious salvation in Christ. Our lives should always reflect the love and holiness of Jesus, so that the people around us, especially unbelievers, can recognize that we are followers of Jesus (Acts 4:13).

Indeed, we need the gospel every moment so that we can continue to live faithfully for Christ. As an unknown preacher once noted, "There are two parts to the Gospel. The first part is believing it, and the second part is behaving it." There is a sense in which we must evangelize ourselves regularly, not for our salvation, obviously, but for our ongoing sanctification. We who have already been saved by grace through faith in Christ must continue proclaiming the gospel to ourselves for our own conformity to the image of Christ. In the words of Jerry Bridges (1929–2016), we should "preach the gospel to ourselves every day and learn to live by it."[5] If we fail to preach the gospel to ourselves and live by it, we will increasingly become legalistic in our thinking and behavior, just as the Pharisees did in the New Testament. This is because "gospel truth is the only root whereon gospel holiness will grow," as the Puritan theologian John Owen (1616–1683) explained.[6]

What Is the Gospel?

The second term that I want to clarify is *gospel*. This word is constantly being used by Christians, but what exactly does it mean? We can answer this by comparing two related passages of Scripture. In Mark 1:15, Jesus urges his listeners to "Repent, and believe in the gospel" with the understood implication that, by doing so, they will be saved. However, in Acts 16:30–31, the Philippian jailer inquires of Paul and Silas, "Sirs, what must I do to be saved?" to which they reply, "Believe on the Lord Jesus Christ, and you will be saved...."

While Jesus teaches that people must "believe in the gospel" to be saved, Paul and Silas instruct the jailer to "believe on the Lord Jesus Christ" to be saved. Here, we see that the expressions *believe in the gospel* and *believe on the Lord Jesus Christ* are essentially synonymous with one another. This means the gospel *is* Jesus Christ and Jesus Christ *is* the gospel!

---

5. Jerry Bridges, *The Discipline of Grace: God's Role and Our Role in the Pursuit of Holiness* (Colorado Springs: NavPress, 1994), 46.

6. John Owen, *The Golden Book of John Owen*, ed. James Moffatt (London: Hodder and Stoughton, 1904), 137.

Therefore, to proclaim the gospel is to proclaim Christ, and to reject the gospel is to reject Christ. The gospel is all about the person and work of Jesus—that He was born to fulfill the law's demand (which is perfect obedience, a demand we all failed to meet) and that He died to pay sin's penalty, which is death (a penalty we all deserve for transgressing God's law). Indeed, Jesus kept the law on behalf of sinners and died in their place, so that sinners who believe in Him will be justified on the basis of His perfect obedience or righteousness. That is, they will be legally declared righteous as if they had never sinned before and as if they had perfectly obeyed God's law (Rom. 5:19). As a result, those who have repented of their sins and have believed the gospel now "have peace with God" (v. 1). Moreover, there is "now no condemnation to those who are in Christ Jesus" (8:1).

My point is this: The historical and biblical Jesus is the embodiment of the gospel (1 Cor. 15:1–4)! Imagine, then, the implication that is made when believers say that they no longer need to hear the gospel because they are already saved. Such an assertion suggests that they no longer need to hear Christ anymore, either! However, all sinners, both saved and unsaved, will always need Christ, who is our all in all (Col. 3:11). Believers need Jesus just as much as unbelievers do. Therefore, all believers must continue to proclaim Christ to themselves and others. Unfortunately, some Christians think of evangelism—the glorious work of *every* Christian to share the gospel with others—as being *only* for pastors and those specifically called to be missionaries or evangelists. They believe that as long as they are active members of their churches and are serving God in *some* way, they have no need to share the gospel with people who are spiritually lost. After all, they reason, God can save sinners however He chooses to do so, with or without our participation. But, as will be further explained in this book, God is pleased to use sinners, such as we are, for the spread of the gospel throughout the world.

In 1789, William Carey (1761–1834)—considered by some to be "the Father and Founder of Modern Missions"[7]—attended a meeting of Baptist ministers in England. In that meeting he stood up and explained the obligation of the church to spread the gospel throughout the world. One of the pastors in the meeting told him, "Sit down, young man; when God wants to convert the heathen, He'll do it without your help or mine."[8] The pastor was suggesting that we have no need to *intentionally* reach pagans with the gospel; after all, if God intends to save them, He will bring them to the gospel in some supernatural way, or bring the gospel to them without our assistance. But this is not the attitude that Scripture teaches us to have!

Thankfully, Carey did not sit down; he did not listen to this pastor, who at that time represented the

---

7. John Brown Myers, *William Carey: The Shoemaker Who Became "the Father and Founder of Modern Missions"* (Leopold Classic Library, 2016).

8. William Carey, *An Enquiry into the Obligations of Christians, to Use Means for the Conversion of the Heathens* (Leicester: Ann Ireland, 1792), iii.

attitude of many Calvinistic Baptists toward evangelism. Instead, in 1792, Carey penned *An Enquiry into the Obligations of Christians to Use Means for the Conversion of the Heathens*. In this treatise, Carey argues how the Great Commission, given by our Lord to His disciples in Matthew 28:19–20, is still binding on us today, and that we should use every lawful means to share the gospel of Jesus Christ throughout the world. Later that same year, with the help of his other like-minded ministers such as John Sutcliff (1752–1814), John Ryland Jr. (1753–1825), Andrew Fuller (1754–1815), and Samuel Pearce (1766–1799), Carey founded the Particular [or Calvinistic] Baptist Society for Propagating the Gospel Among the Heathen, which was later renamed the Baptist Missionary Society. Then in 1793, the year after the foundation of this society, Carey sailed for India with his wife and children to propagate the gospel of Jesus Christ among the heathens there.

God may not require you to do just what Carey did—leave your home and engage in foreign missions—since not all Christians share this same divine calling, but if you strongly sense God's call for you to be a missionary either locally or internationally, then, by all means, go wherever God leads you! Even if you don't have this calling, though, you are still instructed by God to engage in His work of evangelism. Indeed, you are still required to share the gospel with unbelievers, calling them to repent of their sins and trust in Jesus Christ for their eternal salvation. Please allow me, then, to offer five reasons why *all* believers must evangelize.

CHAPTER TWO

Five Reasons Why All Christians Must Evangelize

[If they] fail to talk about Jesus Christ, they are to me tombstones and graves of the dead.
—IGNATIUS OF ANTIOCH

Here are five reasons why you and I both must be actively involved in the work of evangelism.

1. Evangelism Is a Way of Life

In the book of Acts, evangelism is shown to be a regular practice among Christians. Acts 8:4 says, "Therefore those [believers] who were scattered [because of persecution] went everywhere preaching the word." The Greek word which is translated here as "preaching" (*euangelizo*) can also be translated as "evangelizing." Thus, in this context "preaching the word" means proclaiming the gospel. And in this passage the persecuted believers were ordinary Christians (not ordained pastors). Whenever God gave them an opportunity, they shared the message of the cross with unbelievers—even amid persecution! They evangelized wherever they went, because they understood evangelism to be a vital part of their lives in Christ. Evangelism was a way of life for them.

As followers of Christ in our own day, we should imitate their example of faithful Christian living and regard evangelism as a part of our daily lives, too. Wherever we are—whether we are home, at church, at school, at work, at the bank, at the restaurant, at the airport, at the gym, at the hospital, at the store, at the hairdresser, or anywhere else!—let us seize every opportunity that God gives to us to present the gospel to others. Whenever God opens a door for us to talk about His Son, let us grab it, because we may not have this opportunity again. For example, you may not meet again the unbelieving passenger sitting right next to you on the plane. Of course, if after having tried to reach out to him with the gospel, you sense that the passenger does not want to converse with you, you should respect that. At least, you have tried your best to gospelize him. Our problem today is that many Christians do not even attempt to evangelize. They just waste the obvious opportunity that God gives to them. Even a simple "May God bless you" to a cashier at the store or the response "God is good to me" to a waiter's "How are you?" question can spark a conversation or plant a seed in the ear of the hearer.

Dear believer, is evangelism a way of life for you? Is it part of your daily life? Do you evangelize regularly? When was the last time you shared the gospel with others? Do you take every opportunity that God gives to you to tell others about the reason Jesus came into this world: "to seek and to save that which was lost" (Luke 19:10)?

2. Evangelism Is Part of Our Identity in Christ

Evangelism is inextricably tied to our identity as Christians. Question 32 of the Heidelberg Catechism asks, "But why are you called a Christian?" and then answers, "Because by faith I am a member of Christ (Acts 11:26; 1 John 2:27) and thus share in His anointing (Acts 2:17)."[1] Jesus, the Son of God, is ordained by the Father and anointed with His Spirit to be our chief Prophet, High Priest, and eternal King. In Christ, we become partakers of His anointing. That is, we become prophets, priests, and kings. Yes, if you are a Christian, you are also one of God's prophets! We are prophets in the sense that we proclaim God's Word to others. To prophesy in this sense is simply to proclaim God's message. This is how the term "prophesy" is used in Ezekiel 37:4, where God says to Ezekiel, "Prophesy to these bones, and say to them, 'O dry bones, hear the word of the Lord!'" Here God is asking Ezekiel to evangelize these dry bones, which symbolically refer to the spiritually dead people of Israel (v. 11).

Now, going back to the idea of Christians as prophets; since the main point of the whole Bible is Jesus Christ (John 1:45; 5:39; Luke 24:44), our ultimate

---

1. The Heidelberg Catechism (1563) in *Reformed Confessions of the 16th and 17th Centuries in English Translation: Vol. 2, 1552–1566*, compiled with introductions by James T. Dennison Jr. (Grand Rapids: Reformation Heritage Books, 2010), 777.

work, then, as prophets is to point others to Jesus, who is the living *logos* or eternal Word of God (John 1:1–2). Such a work, the pointing of sinners to Christ in whom alone salvation can be found, is at the very heart of evangelism. Remember, we have said earlier that an evangelist is someone who proclaims Jesus Christ. Therefore, in this context, to be a prophet and to be an evangelist are two different terms that have the same basic meaning, since both have the goal to proclaim Christ.

In Christ, we are prophets and so we proclaim God's message; or in Christ, we are evangelists and so we present the gospel. To put it another way, we proclaim Jesus because we are prophets, or we evangelize because we are evangelists. In short, evangelism is our identity in Christ. Wherever we go, we should then remind ourselves of what we are in Christ—prophets or evangelists—and we should never be ashamed of this identity, which our loving Savior gives to us! Sadly, many Christians do not realize that evangelism is part of their identity in Christ. Consequently, they do not evangelize. They think that the proclamation of the gospel is a work that belongs exclusively to pastors or missionaries. Wrong! If you are a Christian, you are an evangelist and are thus expected to do the glorious work of evangelism. The question is do you evangelize? Once you become consciously aware of your identity in Christ as a gospelist, by God's grace evangelism will become a way of life for you.

3. Evangelism Arises from Our Love for Unbelievers

Jesus commands us, "You shall love your neighbor as yourself" (Matt. 22:39). How then can we say that we love our neighbors, especially our unbelieving neighbors, if we do not share the gospel with them? If we were to see our neighbor's house burning in the middle of the night, how would we choose to express our love for him? Depending on the precise situation, calling 911 on his behalf might be the most helpful thing that we can do. If we were able, though, it might be even more helpful for us to run toward our neighbor's house and shout, "Hey, get out of your house! It's on fire!" In other words, if we are really concerned about the well-being of our neighbor, we will make every effort to give him our best help and to minister to his most urgent need.

Unbelievers are much like our neighbor in this illustration. If they remain unrepentant of their sins and disbelieving in Christ, they will suffer forever in the lake of fire (Rev. 21:8). Yet if we really love them, as God repeatedly commands us to do, then we should feel *compelled* to share the gospel with them—and to help them understand that if they genuinely repent of their sins and believe in the Lord Jesus Christ, they will not perish in hell, but have everlasting life in heaven (John 3:16). How loving are we if we do not share this marvelous message with the people around us?

Another helpful illustration is that of a neighbor who is dying of a particular illness. We have knowledge of a cure that can save them. In this situation, would we allow shyness, fear, or perhaps even apathy to prevent us from telling others about the cure? No! Likewise, should we allow anything to prevent us from telling unbelievers about Jesus? If so, we would be disobeying God's Word and dishonoring God Himself. Yet this is precisely the situation that we are currently in with regard to the gospel, which has been entrusted to us for both *keeping* (guarding against attack and misrepresentation) and *sharing* (1 Thess. 2:4).

Just as we could never in good conscience allow our neighbors to die from a house fire about which we can warn them or from a disease for which we have the cure, so we should not let them pass from this life without hearing some proclamation of the gospel of Christ! If we genuinely care for those who are lost, we will surely pray for their salvation and give our best to help them see that they are perishing without Christ. A love for our "neighbor" compels us to do this.

Dear Christian, do you really love your neighbors, especially your unbelieving ones? Do they see and feel God's love in you? Do they even know you are a Christian? When was the last time you visited your neighbors and talked to them about the gospel? Don't wait for them to come to you to hear the gospel; go to them and show them how much you care for them. Unfortunately, after the September 11 attacks and with an increasing number of crimes in our society today, some people have become extremely cautious to the point that they will not entertain any strangers. That can be why door-to-door evangelism is not an effective method nowadays. There is therefore a need for us Christians to earn the trust of our neighbors and establish a good relationship with them before we can talk to them about the gospel. Of course, there are many ways to cultivate friendship with them. Perhaps we can invite them for supper (hospitality), or bring cookies to them, or help them rake their leaves, or shovel their snow. The examples can go on and on. The point is we need to take the initiative to reach out to them with the gospel. What kind of effort do you make to build a bridge between you and your neighbors so you can bring the gospel to them? In his *The Saints' Everlasting Rest*, the Puritan pastor Richard Baxter (1615–1691) captured well my point here:

> Oh, if you have the hearts of Christians...let them yearn toward your poor, ignorant, ungodly and neighbors,...if they die unregenerate, they are lost forever. Have you hearts of rock, that cannot pity men in such a case? If you believe not the word of God, how are you Christians yourselves? If you do but believe it, why do you not bestir you [or start being active] to help others? Do you not care who is damned, so you be saved?... Has God had so much mercy on you, and will you have no mercy on your poor neighbors?... Have you not a neighbor that sets his heart below, and neglects eternity? What blessed place do you live in, where there is none such? If there be not some of them in your own family, it is well; and yet are you silent? Do you live close by them, or meet them in the streets, or labor with them, or travel with them, or sit still and talk with them, and say nothing to them of their souls, or the life to come?[2]

---

2. Richard Baxter, *The Saints' Everlasting Rest* (Philadelphia:

4. Evangelism Originates in the Very Nature of Our God

God Himself is an evangelist. In Luke 2:10–11, God's angel (or heavenly messenger) evangelizes the shepherds on God's behalf, saying: "Do not be afraid, for behold, I bring you good tidings of great joy which will be to all people. For there is born to you this day in the city of David a Savior, who is Christ the Lord." So when we evangelize, we imitate God, who is the great Evangelist—who created us, loves us, and commands us to grow increasingly into the likeness of His Son. In fact, the only reason we are even able to evangelize is because God evangelized us first! 1 John 4:10 reminds us, "In this is love, not that we loved God, but that He loved us and sent His Son to be the propitiation for our sins." Then John adds, "We love Him because He first loved us" (v. 19). Without God loving us first and pursuing us in such a way, we would all be destined for hell! Yet God loves us unconditionally, and takes the initiative to draw us to Himself, so that, in Christ, we may be eternally saved.

Therefore, it is a tremendous honor and blessing that God uses us to be part of His saving work here on earth—and we should not neglect this privilege to honor Him by telling others about His marvelous love. Paul says, "But God demonstrates His own love toward us, in that while we were still sinners, Christ died for us" (Rom. 5:8). Imagine, out of His

---

Prichard & Hall, 1790), 232–33. Spelling of the quote has been modernized.

unconditional love for us, He "did not spare His own Son, but delivered Him up for us all" (8:32). He did not spare His Son, so He could spare us. What an amazing love our heavenly Father has for us!

Now, while evangelism *begins* with God Himself, we should also acknowledge that it *ends* with Him, too! In other words, it is God who saves people—not we. You may be the one to plant the seed of the gospel, and others may be the ones to water it, but it is always God who brings growth (1 Cor. 3:7). After all, can we—in our limited abilities—save the people around us from eternal judgment? Absolutely not! God alone sovereignly elects those who are to be saved and draws them to Himself through the power of the Holy Spirit for their salvation. Nonetheless, God has been pleased to use us to bring this to pass. Though God does not tell us in advance whom He will ultimately save, He instructs us to share His good news with all people and to be faithful in evangelizing, knowing that only He can truly accomplish salvation in the hearts of lost sinners. God is delighted to use both the gospel (or evangel) and the gospelist (or evangelist) to save sinners.

5. Evangelism Is a Command As Set Forth in the Great Commission

Consider the familiar but profoundly significant instructions of our Lord in Matthew 28:18–20:

> And Jesus came and spoke to them, saying, "All authority has been given to Me in heaven and on earth. Go therefore and make disciples of all the nations, baptizing them in the name of the Father

and of the Son and of the Holy Spirit, teaching them to observe all things that I have commanded you; and lo, I am with you always, even to the end of the age." Amen.

Now, we cannot "make disciples of all the nations," unless we first proclaim the gospel to them. The unbelievers must first be converted to Christ before they can be His disciples or followers. The parallel passage in Mark 16:15 makes this clear by instructing us to "Go into all the world and preach the gospel to every creature." Evangelism is the crucial first step in making disciples for Christ, for people cannot fruitfully grow in their understanding of God's Word until they first encounter the God who so lovingly gave that Word to them. Therefore, we must be evangelizing on a regular basis if we are to obey Christ's command to make disciples in the Great Commission.

Evangelism is not something that should cause us to boast, though—God fully expects us to evangelize in obedience to Him. Paul writes, "For if I preach the gospel, I have nothing to boast of, for necessity is laid upon me; yes, woe is me if I do not preach the gospel!" (1 Cor. 9:16). Likewise, Paul says in Romans 1:14–15, "I am a debtor both to Greeks and to barbarians, both to wise and to unwise. So, as much as is in me, I am ready to preach the gospel to you who are in Rome also." Paul recognizes how God has worked through others to help him in his own faith journey; and he concludes that, ultimately, it is God to whom all credit is due regarding salvation, since God alone is the author and perfecter of our faith (Heb. 12:2). In agreeing to preach the gospel in Rome, where the church was already established, Paul was also acknowledging that the gospel is not merely for the lost who need to be saved, but also for growing Christians who need to be freshly encouraged in their devotion to Christ.

Priscilla J. Owens (1829–1907) wrote a beautiful hymn that we still love to sing; it is titled "Jesus Saves" (but also known as "We Have Heard the Joyful Sound"). The lyrics serve to remind us of our all-important task as Christians:

> We have heard the joyful sound:
> Jesus saves! Jesus saves!
> Spread the tidings all around:
> Jesus saves! Jesus saves!
> Bear the news to ev'ry land,
> Climb the steeps and cross the waves;
> Onward! 'tis our Lord's command;
> Jesus saves! Jesus saves![3]

Note, it is our Lord's command to spread the good tidings all around. Or as William Shedd contends, "It is the duty of the Christian Church to preach the gospel to every creature, because Christ the Head of the Church has commanded it so to do. It follows from this, that every individual member is obliged to contribute to this result, in proportion to his means and opportunity."[4]

Nevertheless, please understand that this point

---

3. Priscilla J. Owens, "Jesus Saves," accessed November 23, 2023, https://hymnary.org/text/we_have_heard_the_joyful_sound.

4. Shedd, "Success of Evangelistic Labor," in *Sermons to the Spiritual Man* (New York: Charles Scribner's Sons, 1884), 400.

about evangelism being a divine command for us to obey is placed last in my list, though we might be tempted to place it first. While it's crucial for us to remember that God does, indeed, *command* us to share the gospel by good and necessary consequence, I placed it last here for a very specific reason—I don't want you to share the gospel out of *guilt*, but out of *gratitude* for what God has done for you in Jesus Christ. We are never to proclaim God's message of salvation as militant soldiers simply doing what's demanded of us. Instead, it should be out of love for God and love for our neighbor that we eagerly, prayerfully, and joyfully seek out opportunities to share the gospel with others.

If a husband were to bring home flowers, chocolates, and a beautiful card for his wife, would it matter if he later confessed to buying these things for her out of duty—to simply *obey* what God's Word commands that he do as a husband? Yes, it would matter! The wife's desire is not simply to receive tangible gifts from her husband, but—far more important—to know that whatever gifts that he might give to her are given because he loves her, cherishes her, and wants to express his delight in her and his gratitude for all that she means to him. In the same way, we should not evangelize out of a sense of guilt or duty, which doesn't honor God in the appropriate way, but out of our genuine love for God, our joy in knowing Him, our gratitude for the multitude of ways that He blesses our lives each day, and out of our deep desire that other people might come to know Him as we have.

We should remember another beloved hymn that expresses these convictions so well—"I Love to Tell the Story," by Katherine Hankey (1834–1911):

> I love to tell the story, because I know 'tis true;
> It satisfies my longings as nothing else can do.[5]

In other words, Hankey is evangelizing because it satisfies her longings, and it brings her delight. Indeed, evangelism brings joy to the faithful Christian, but it also brings joy to the angels in heaven, and to our triune God whenever we do this! "I say to you," says Jesus, "there is joy in the presence of the angels of God over one sinner who repents" (Luke 15:10). Please ask yourself this: When was the last time you experienced this kind of joy, the joy that flows out of the work of evangelism? We can't wait to tell others about the good things that have happened to us. But what about the happiness that should come from our relationship to God? Do we have the same zeal for sharing about God's amazing love? We should!

The hymn continues:

> I love to tell the story; it did so much for me;
> And that is just the reason I tell it now to thee.[6]

All of us who are children of God should be able to echo these sentiments in our own hearts as we reflect on how knowing God has changed our lives in such significant ways. The gospel has done so much for us;

---

5. Katherine Hankey, "I Love to Tell the Story," accessed November 23, 2023, https://www.hymnal.net/en/hymn/h/1064.

6. Hankey, "I Love to Tell the Story."

Jesus has done so much for us! Christ gave His life for us; He died on the cross to save us from the power and penalty of sin! We should have been in hell a long time ago, but here we are, still alive and now free from the bondage of sin and Satan! Jesus has done literally *so much* for us, and that should be more than enough to motivate us to evangelize—not out of guilt, but out of gratitude, not merely out of duty, but out of delight for what God has done for us in the gospel.

Of course, we all have excuses for not evangelizing; we all come up with legitimate-sounding alibis to justify our failure to tell others about Christ. In fact, I'm going to "help you" in your excuse-making by offering five popular reasons that believers often give for not evangelizing. At the same time, though, I'm also going to share what I believe are God's answers to our excuses. My end goal is to help us to see the foolishness of our excuses and to recognize our need to evangelize in spite of them.

CHAPTER THREE

Five Excuses Some Christians Use for Not Evangelizing

"Come now, therefore, and I will send you to Pharaoh that you may bring My people, the children of Israel, out of Egypt." But Moses said to God, "Who am I that I should go to Pharaoh, and that I should bring the children of Israel out of Egypt?" So He said, "I will certainly be with you. And this shall be a sign to you that I have sent you: When you have brought the people out of Egypt, you shall serve God on this mountain." Then Moses said to God, "Indeed, when I come to the children of Israel and say to them, 'The God of your fathers has sent me to you,' and they say to me, 'What is His name?' what shall I say to them?" And God said to Moses, "I AM WHO I AM." And He said, "Thus you shall say to the children of Israel, 'I AM has sent me to you.'"

Then Moses answered and said, "But suppose they will not believe me or listen to my voice; suppose they say, 'The LORD has not appeared to you.'" So the LORD said to him, "What is that in your hand?" He said, "A rod." And He said, "Cast it on the ground." So he cast it on the ground, and it became a serpent; and Moses fled from it. Then the LORD said to Moses, "Reach out your hand and take it by the tail" (and he reached out his hand and caught it, and it became a rod in his hand), "that they may believe that the LORD God of their fathers, the God of Abraham, the God of Isaac, and the God of Jacob, has appeared to you."

Then Moses said to the Lord, "O my Lord, I am not eloquent, neither before nor since You have spoken to Your servant; but I am slow of speech and slow of tongue." So the LORD said to him, "Who has made man's mouth? Or who makes the mute, the deaf, the seeing, or the blind? Have not I, the LORD? Now therefore, go, and I will be with your mouth and teach you what you shall say." But he said, "O my Lord, please send by the hand of whomever else You may send." So the anger of the LORD was kindled against Moses, and He said: "Is not Aaron the Levite your brother? I know that he can speak well. And look, he is also coming out to meet you. When he sees you, he will be glad in his heart. Now you shall speak to him and put the words in his mouth. And I will be with your mouth and with his mouth, and I will teach you what you shall do. So he shall be your spokesman to the people. And he himself shall be as a mouth for you, and you shall be to him as God. And you shall take this rod in your hand, with which you shall do the signs."
—Exodus 3:10–14; 4:1–5, 10–17

Here are five excuses we sometimes use for not doing the work of evangelism.

1. I Am Not Worthy; Who Am I?
When God commands Moses to go before Pharaoh, the first excuse, which Moses offers in the form of a question, is "Who am I that I should go to Pharaoh,

and that I should bring the children of Israel out of Egypt?" (Exod. 3:11). Today, we often express this same concern ourselves, saying, "I know that I'm supposed to share the gospel, but *who am I* to do this?" Perhaps what Moses is saying here is, "Why are you sending *me*? I am weak. Pharaoh is strong and you want *me* to go to him?" Notice, however, what God tells Moses in verse 12: "I will certainly be with you." What an encouraging promise! God is telling Moses, "Yes, I know you are weak, but *I* will be with you!"

You might be using this same excuse today. Perhaps you're saying something like this to God: "I am shy or an introvert." "I am weak." "I have no formal theological training." "I am afraid." And you're asking God, "Who am I that you would send me out to evangelize?" But remember what Jesus tells us in Matthew 28:20: "Lo, I am with you always, even to the end of the age." We do not do the work of evangelism alone! God is with us!

David Livingstone (1813–1873), a Scottish missionary who traveled to Africa and helped open one-third of the continent to Christian missions, came to cherish Matthew 28:20 as his "life verse." After some difficult years of ministry in Africa, he returned to Scotland to share publicly about the ministry that he'd done. When he was asked whether he would be willing to return to Africa to do additional work, he offered the following reply:

> [W]ould you like me to tell you what supported me through all the years of exile among people whose language I could not understand, and

whose attitude towards me was always uncertain and often hostile? It was this: *"Lo, I am with you alway[s], even unto the end of the world!"* On those words I staked everything, and they never failed![1]

Livingstone found comfort in this verse, knowing that he could go wherever the Lord led him because the Lord would always be with him. In the same way, God will be with us, too—not just some of the time, but *all* the time! So, be comforted, dear brothers and sisters, and know that whenever we set out to do the Lord's work, He goes with us as our guide and our comfort in all that we do.

Your concern may be, "I'm not well-educated," but you don't have to be a scholar to share your faith with others, for the God who knows *all* things goes with you! Consider also Acts 4, in which Peter and John are preaching the gospel and leading thousands of people to Christ, but the skeptical religious leaders confront them, asking who gave them the power and authority to do this. After explaining that Jesus, who had been raised from the dead, was their authority, the leaders were amazed. Note their reaction in verse 13: "Now when they saw the boldness of Peter and John, and perceived that they were uneducated and untrained men, they marveled. And they realized that they had been with Jesus." Peter and John were not well-educated men, yet God used that to demonstrate His power. In the same way, God can use each of us

---

1. Cited in F. W. Boreham, "David Livingstone's Life Text," accessed November 23, 2023, http://www.wholesomewords.org/missions/bliving8.html.

to spread the message of the cross, despite our own particular shortcomings, and promises to be with us as we serve Him (1 Cor. 1:27).

2. I Do Not Know What to Say

This excuse is used in Exodus 3:13:

> Then Moses said to God, "Indeed, when I come to the children of Israel and say to them, 'The God of your fathers has sent me to you,' and they say to me, 'What is His name?' what shall I say to them?"

Please note, while Moses's first concern was about defending himself to Pharaoh, this second excuse is regarding his ability to establish his authority with the Israelites themselves. Moses is contemplating his interaction with different people—the Egyptian ruler whose authority he will be challenging as well as the people of God whom he's being called to rescue. Like us, Moses tried to consider every potential problem with the call that God had given to him!

The question is one that's easy for us to identify with—"What shall I say?" In other words, if the people to whom we are sent start asking us questions about God, inquiring as to whether we truly know and represent Him, what can we say to demonstrate that we *do*?

In Moses's case, the answer is given in the verse that follows: "And God said to Moses, 'I AM WHO I AM.' And He said, 'Thus you shall say to the children of Israel, I AM has sent me to you'" (Exod. 3:14). In identifying Himself as "I AM," God is reminding us that He is the faithful, covenant-keeping God who does not change. God always has been and always will be, and His Word is true today, just as it has always been true. Therefore, we can fully trust in Him as He guides us, knowing that all that He says is true, and that future events will always come to pass according to His sovereign plan.

One of the reasons that we try so hard to avoid evangelism is that we want to make the gospel more complicated than it actually is. The gospel is simple! We should learn this lesson from the example of Paul and Silas, who—as we've already mentioned—told the Philippian jailer, "Believe on the Lord Jesus Christ, and you will be saved...." There's no mention here of the two disciples insisting that the jailer first study the Old Testament and be able to clearly articulate how Jesus was the fulfillment of the prophecy. They did not insist the jailer sit under their teaching for a set amount of time before putting his faith in Jesus. No—Paul and Silas simply told the Philippian jailer that if he would believe on the Lord Jesus Christ, he would be saved. *That* is the simple gospel message. In evangelism, we do not need to explain the Five Points of Calvinism or make sure the hearer first subscribes to the Three Forms of Unity: The Belgic Confession of Faith, the Canons of Dort, and the Heidelberg Catechism (helpful though these statements of faith are!).

We can also learn this lesson directly from our Lord's example. When the thief on the cross spoke to Jesus (in Luke 23:42) and petitioned "Lord, remember me when You come into Your kingdom," Jesus did not correct him by saying, "I'm sorry, but you must specifically say, 'Lord save me from the power and penalty of my sin,' or I won't be able to do anything for you." Jesus never corrected him because He knew precisely what the thief was asking. The response that Jesus gave was simply "today you will be with Me in Paradise" (v. 43).

In evangelism, we are simply announcing the Good News—we are not teaching systematic theology or lecturing about church history or the five *solas* of the Reformation; and we are certainly not trying to discern for ourselves whether or not that person we evangelize is one of the elect of God. Please don't do that when evangelizing! Instead, use the approach which Paul and Silas used—simply tell people that if they believe on the Lord Jesus Christ, they *will* be saved! Why? Because that is what God calls us to do as we share the gospel with lost people—and because the power of conviction comes not from our ability to persuade, but from God Himself, and from His gospel message. That is why, in Romans 1:16, Paul writes, "For I am not ashamed of the gospel of Christ, for it is the power of God to salvation for everyone who believes."

Having said this, it does not mean that you do not need to present the gospel message *clearly* and *compellingly*. With the Holy Spirit's help, persuade your listeners that they are sinners, deserving of death, even eternal death in the lake of fire, and that unless they repent of their sins and believe in the Lord Jesus Christ, they will perish in hell. Learn from the apostle Paul, who "reasoned in the synagogue every Sabbath, and persuaded both Jews and Greeks" to believe the gospel (Acts 18:4).

Sometimes, though, in evangelism, all you really need to do is quote a passage from the Bible and pray that God will use that verse to transform the life of the hearer. In 1857, Charles Spurgeon was asked to preach a message at the Crystal Palace. A day or two before preaching there, Spurgeon went to visit the building to test the acoustics of the room and determine where the preaching platform should be. To do this, he simply stood before the seemingly empty room and cried in a loud voice, "Behold! The Lamb of God who takes away the sin of the world!" (John 1:29). Spurgeon later learned that a workman who was in one of the galleries that day heard these words proclaimed, came under the conviction of sin, went home that evening and put his faith in the Lamb of God—simply from hearing Spurgeon cry out a single verse of Scripture![2]

Truly, there's no limit to what God can do, or how He can work miracles from our humble obedience to Him. Don't be discouraged if you haven't formally studied theology. If you know John 3:16, then you have the message! If you know Romans 6:23, then you have the message! You don't need to be a theologian or an apologist to share your faith. The gospel is simple, and we are to keep it simple when we share it with others. Yet, it does not mean you should not "always be ready to give a defense to everyone who asks

---

2. Charles H. Spurgeon, *My Sermon Notes: A Selection from Outlines of Discourses Delivered at the Metropolitan Tabernacle with Anecdotes and Illustrations* (New York: Funk & Wagnalls, 1890), 231.

you a reason for the hope that is in you" (1 Pet. 3:15). And if by God's grace the person you evangelized believed the gospel, then as God enables you, disciple this new convert by helping him "grow in the grace and knowledge of our Lord and Savior Jesus Christ" (2 Pet. 3:18). This is the appropriate time to teach him more about theology, church history, and spiritual disciplines (such as worship and prayer) that will strengthen his faith in Christ.

3. They Will Not Believe Me

Exodus 4:1 states, "Then Moses answered and said, But suppose they will not believe me or listen to my voice; suppose they say, The LORD has not appeared to you." God's kindness in responding to this protest is a tremendous demonstration of His grace and mercy toward Moses—and toward us—for it's a direct contradiction of what God had already declared to be true! In Exodus 3:18, God had already explained to Moses that "they will heed your voice; and you shall come, you and the elders of Israel." But, with his very next words, Moses expressed his unbelief in what God had just said! Rather than responding in righteous anger, however, the Lord graciously offered Moses a quick demonstration of His miracle-working power (Exod. 4:2–9), so as to give Moses assurance that, even in the face of opposition among the Egyptians, God's miracles would substantiate the words that Moses was to speak.

In raising this concern, Moses is essentially saying, "Okay, Lord, now I know that you will be with me, and I know what I should say, but the people to whom you are sending me still won't believe me." This makes me want to say to Moses, "Have you even tried? God clearly told you that Israel would listen, but you're already convinced that the people won't listen to you! Try it first! You're so pessimistic, Moses!"

I'm afraid that, just like Moses, we too are pessimistic about simply doing what God asks us to or going where God sends us. We have a never-ending list of worries, fears, and "what if" questions; and we let them keep us from doing God's will. Sometimes we'll say things like, "I don't want to talk to my unbelieving neighbors or relatives about Jesus, because they won't believe what I tell them." When I hear believers say that, I want to ask, "Have you tried? How do you know they won't believe in Christ? Are you so pessimistic about God's willingness and ability to save sinners?"

We should first go where God sends and do as He has instructed. Then, if the people still don't believe us—so what? Our faithfulness is determined by our obedience to God's commands, and nothing more. It is not our duty to make others believe the gospel; that is the work of the Holy Spirit! We might wish that we *could* make others believe in Christ, for their own benefit and blessing, but we don't have that ability. Our duty is simply to tell them about Jesus Christ. The people to whom God sends us might have a lot of questions for us. If so, we can help them find the answers that they seek in God's Word. However, we should also remember the old English proverb: "You can lead a horse to water, but you can't make him drink." You cannot make an unbeliever drink from the fountain of life, but what you can do is lead that person to the living water and ask the Holy Spirit to move that person to come to Jesus Christ and be saved. We can also attempt to create a thirst for the gospel, by first establishing a genuine friendship with a lost person and then, at an appropriate time, sharing our personal testimony of faith in Christ. If the other person should ask, "Why are you showing this care and concern for me?", then it presents us with the perfect opportunity to say, "Because the Bible says to love your neighbor as yourself, and I want to share this love that I've found in Jesus Christ, so that you can experience it for yourself."

Here in the passages from Exodus we see the balance between divine sovereignty and human responsibility. Admittedly, some believers will try to use God's sovereignty as an excuse for not evangelizing, saying, "I am a strong believer in God's sovereignty, and in the doctrine of election, and I know that the Bible tells us (in Ephesians 1:4) that before the foundation of the world God has chosen some to be saved. So, I trust that—in God's time—He will bring some of those elect sinners to our church."

Oh, my friend, you are dead wrong if you think like the above-mentioned believer! This is the problem with hyper-Calvinism, which emphasizes the sovereignty of God to the extreme, leading to a complete denial of our God-ordained responsibility as His people to share the gospel with sinners. On August 1, 1858,

Charles Spurgeon preached a sermon titled, "Sovereign Grace and Man's Responsibility," in which he said, "You ask me to reconcile the two [that is, divine sovereignty and human responsibility]. I answer, they do not want [i.e., need] any reconcilement; I never tried to reconcile them to myself, because I could never see a discrepancy.... Both are true; no two truths can be inconsistent with each other; and what you have to do is to believe them both."[3] Spurgeon recognized—as we should—that while we can't save anybody in our own limited abilities (not even ourselves!), God has nonetheless chosen to use us to proclaim the gospel throughout the world. What an honor it is that God calls us to participate in the building of His kingdom on earth like this—and how foolish it would be of us to neglect such a blessed opportunity!

Some people believe that the doctrine of election is an enemy of biblical evangelism, but it is not. In fact, this doctrine is our encouragement as we evangelize! For, if there were no election, there would be no guarantee for us that spiritually dead sinners could ever be made alive in Christ. The fact that God has already chosen to save *some* before the foundation of the world should motivate us to go out and reach the lost, knowing that some people will surely be saved!

Our job, however, is not to attempt to recognize the elect from the non-elect—as if we are even able to

---

3. Charles Spurgeon, "Sovereign Grace and Man's Responsibility," accessed December 5, 2023, https://www.spurgeon.org/resource-library/sermons/sovereign-grace-and-mans-responsibility/#flipbook/.

do so—but to proclaim the gospel to all lost sinners, and to pray for their salvation, trusting in God to ultimately save those whom He chooses to save. Even Jesus proclaimed the gospel in this way, inviting all who heard Him to respond in faith. In Matthew 11:28, Jesus addresses a large and diverse crowd of people, saying, "Come to Me, all you who labor and are heavy laden, and I will give you rest." Jesus knew (as He states in John 6:44) that only those whom the Father draws will ever respond to His call, but that did not prevent Him from calling all people to repent and trust in Him. We must learn from the example set by our Lord—the gospel is to be proclaimed to *all* people, and it's to be shared faithfully, with the understanding that only God Himself is truly able to save!

4. I Am Not Eloquent

Moses uses this excuse in Exodus 4:10: "Then Moses said to the LORD, 'O my Lord, I am not eloquent, neither before nor since You have spoken to Your servant; but I am slow of speech and slow of tongue.'" Who is eloquent in their speech? I certainly am not! Thankfully, though, the power of God does not depend on our eloquence! In trying to communicate the gospel to others, we may stumble over some words, or perhaps commit some grammatical errors along the way, but so be it! We serve a sovereign God who can overrule our mistakes—or perhaps even *use* our mistakes to accomplish His eternal purpose and plan.

Many people claim that they are so nervous at the thought of evangelism that they don't believe they would even be able to communicate clearly while sharing the gospel with a lost person. If this describes you, then please consider how you would respond if you saw someone drowning in a pool and you didn't know how to swim. Would you feel this same way, arguing that you're so nervous that you can't articulate words, or would you anxiously scream at the top of your voice, "Please, somebody, save this person"? Undoubtedly, in a situation like this, you wouldn't care about your speaking skills; you probably wouldn't even care a great deal about your own life. Most likely, your only concern at that moment would be for the person who was drowning and urgently needed to be saved.

Of course, this serves to illustrate the evangelistic process, as well. All around us, we see people drowning in sin. Do we care that these people are perishing in such a way? We certainly should! There's little doubt, though, that one of the main reasons that we don't evangelize is that we simply don't care about others—certainly not to the degree that Scripture tells us to.

We think of our families as well as ourselves, but we fall tragically short in our concern for the people to whom we aren't related and are even less concerned about those we don't personally know. Yet, according to Scripture, every person who dies outside of Christ will experience God's wrath in hell forever (2 Thess. 1:9). Therefore, we should take time to contemplate the biblical teaching about hell and allow this disturbing reality to give us a greater concern to overcome our hesitation or embarrassment and engage in evangelism.

God provides the following response to Moses's concern regarding his speaking ability: "So the LORD said to him, 'Who has made man's mouth? Or who makes the mute, the deaf, the seeing, or the blind? Have not I, the LORD? Now therefore, go, and I will be with your mouth and teach you what you shall say'" (Exod. 4:11–12). In Luke 12:11–12, Jesus offers similar counsel to His disciples: "Now when they bring you to the synagogues and magistrates and authorities, do not worry about how or what you should answer, or what you should say. For the Holy Spirit will teach you in that very hour what you ought to say."

At many times in my own life, I have experienced God working in this way. On one occasion, I was sharing my faith with an atheist who had many questions for me, and I was just amazed that, by God's grace, I was able to answer his questions. At the end of our conversation, I was so surprised by how the Lord had guided both my thinking and my speech, enabling me to provide the right answers during that challenging conversation. Surely, that was not me. It was the Holy Spirit working in me because of the grace of God. We need to trust God to not only guide us, but also to equip us for all that He sends us to do.

In 1 Corinthians 2:1–4, Paul reminds us yet again that eloquent speech is not a prerequisite for serving Christ:

> And I, brethren, when I came to you, did not come with excellence of speech or of wisdom declaring

to you the testimony of God. For I determined not to know anything among you except Jesus Christ and Him crucified. I was with you in weakness, in fear, and in much trembling. And my speech and my preaching were not with persuasive words of human wisdom, but in demonstration of the Spirit and of power.

How encouraging it should be to all of us to know that God can work through us regardless of our imperfections! A popular quotation declares that, "An evangelist is a nobody who is seeking to tell everybody about Somebody who can help change anybody."[4] So, as one of God's humble "nobodies," each of us should remember that it is not our eloquence that can bring about lasting change in a lost person's life, but rather it is our all-powerful God working through the gospel message which we are all called to share.

5. I Do Not Want to Do It; Please Send Someone Else

Exodus 4:13 mentions, "But he said, 'O my Lord, please send by the hand of whomever else You may send.'" Now we know why Moses has been making all these excuses to the Lord—he simply doesn't want to go. Isn't the same true for us? We don't want to evangelize simply because we don't want to evangelize—and when we don't want to evangelize, we come up with alibis, or reasons that we shouldn't have to serve the Lord in this way. Of course, we might be too embarrassed to admit our reluctance, but

---

4. Cited in Roy B. Zuck, *The Speaker's Quote Book* (Grand Rapids: Kregel, 1997), 133.

this is the reality for many Christians today, and—apparently—it was the reality for Moses, too!

When Moses made this final effort to avoid doing what God commanded him to do, Exodus 4:14 records how "the anger of the LORD was kindled against Moses." Oh, brothers and sisters, let us not wait for the Lord to become angry with us because we make excuses upon excuses! Instead, let us do what He says or go where He sends, willingly, knowing that He will be with us, guiding us and enabling us to serve Him faithfully. In this case, God graciously provided Moses with a helper in the person of Aaron, his brother. As we go out to serve the Lord, we have the added blessing of knowing that the Holy Spirit, who is a far better helper, goes with us—guiding us, convicting us, and bringing us the peace of God even amid our most difficult experiences (John 14:26).

CHAPTER FOUR

Conclusion

Challenge to Unbelievers
If any unbelievers might find their way to this book, I want you to know that you need the gospel. "A throne without the gospel," said John Owen, "is but the devil's dungeon. Wealth without the gospel is fuel for hell. Advancement without the gospel is but a going high to have the greatest fall."[1] So you must believe the gospel, and remember, to believe the gospel is to believe in Jesus as your Savior and Lord. If you don't turn away from your sin and turn to Christ by faith, you will surely be separated from Him for all eternity in a very real and terrible place called hell (2 Thess. 1:9). But God "is longsuffering toward us, not willing that any should perish but that all should come to repentance" (2 Pet. 3:9). He "is gracious and full of compassion, slow to anger and great in mercy" (Ps. 145:8). In fact, He is more willing to forgive you than you are to be forgiven. He "delights in mercy" (Mic. 7:18), meaning that He enjoys forgiving sinners

---

1. Owen, *The Golden Book*, 219.

who ask for forgiveness no matter how big and many their sins are.

Now, you might say, "I want to turn to Christ in repentance, but how can I with all the sin in my life? I simply don't have the ability to come to Jesus by faith." Consider Jesus's visit with a man who had been sick for thirty-eight years, recorded for us in John 5:8–9: "Jesus said to him, 'Rise, take up your bed and walk.' And immediately the man was made well, took up his bed, and walked." Notice the sick man didn't question what Jesus was telling him to do. He didn't say, "Jesus, don't you see I can't walk? Why are you then asking me to rise and walk?" On the contrary, he was immediately made well and responded in obedience to what Jesus had said—he rose, took up his bed, and walked. Likewise, Jesus is commanding you to repent of your sin and believe in Him.

Don't focus on your inability to do what He is asking you to do. Rather, focus on His ability to forgive and save you when you repent and believe. Consider also what Jesus said to His friend Lazarus, who at this time had been dead for four days: "Lazarus, come forth!" or come out of the grave (John 11:43). Some of those who heard Jesus might have thought, "Why would Jesus call a dead person to come out of the grave? Doesn't He realize a dead person cannot hear and thus respond to a command?" Yet, we read in the next verse, "And he who had died came out" (v. 44). In other words, Lazarus heard Jesus's call and responded to it, because Jesus gave him the ability to hear His voice and come out of the grave.

Let me insert here a word to my fellow believers: when we do evangelism, this is essentially what we are doing, too. We are sharing the gospel with people who are spiritually dead in sin, and who cannot save themselves from the power and penalty of sin (Eph. 2:1). How, then, will they believe the gospel if they are dead in sin? Good question! In their own abilities, they are unable to respond to the gospel—just as the sick man did not possess the ability to walk, or to bring about his own healing. But here's the beauty of the gospel: The Christ who says, "Come to Me, all you who labor and are heavy laden, and I will give you rest" (Matt. 11:28) is the same person who will enable us to come to Him by faith. The God who commands us to believe in His Son is the same person who will give us the faith we need to believe. This way, at the end, we must always give all the praise and glory to God. In one of my articles, I explain it this way:

> To call the unbelievers to repent of their sins and believe in Christ may appear illogical. After all, unless God quickens dead souls, they cannot repent and believe, so it would seem to make more sense if God were to open their hearts to the gospel first, before we call them to repentance and faith. While this seems more logical to us, this is not the biblical pattern. For instance, God commanded Ezekiel to proclaim His words to the people of Israel before He regenerated them. "So I prophesied," the prophet wrote, "as he commanded me, and the breath came into them, and they lived" (37:10). Here we learn how God ordinarily uses the proclamation of His Word to regenerate sinners. And while the

unbelievers are spiritually dead — and thus unable in and of themselves to believe — they have nevertheless the duty to believe for their salvation. The gospel message is clear: Believe in the Lord Jesus Christ, and you will be saved (Acts 16:31). No one can expect to be saved unless he or she believes. In fact, just as pastors are commanded to preach the gospel, so unbelievers are commanded to believe the gospel.[2]

So, returning to you, my unbelieving reader, please don't let anything keep you from believing in Jesus. Don't use your inability as an excuse for not doing what He is asking you to do, namely, to come to Him by faith. The hymnwriter Joseph Hart (1712–1768) puts it along these lines:

> Come, ye sinners, poor and needy,
>   weak and wounded, sick and sore;
> Jesus ready stands to save you,
>   full of pity, love, and pow'r.
>
> Come, ye weary, heavy laden,
>   lost and ruined by the fall;
> If you tarry till you're better,
>   you will never come at all.[3]

Challenge to Believers

To the readers who already belong to Christ, please

---

2. Brian G. Najapfour, "Preaching to Persuade," *Tabletalk*, September 2022, https://tabletalkmagazine.com/article/2022/09/preaching-to-persuade/.

3. Joseph Hart, "Come, Ye Sinners, Poor and Needy," accessed November 14, 2023, https://hymnary.org/text/come_ye_sinners_poor_and_needy_weak_and.

stop making unreasonable alibis for not evangelizing! Instead, establish better habits of talking to others about Jesus regularly. Start in "Jerusalem" (in your home). Maybe one of your children is not yet saved, or perhaps your father or mother is not yet a believer. Then, from "Jerusalem" move to "Judea" and "Samaria" (your neighborhood and community), and from there, as the Holy Spirit calls and enables you, go "to the end of the earth" (Acts 1:8). My point is that you present the gospel to those who are lost in sin wherever you are and whenever God gives you an opportunity to do so.

Ask your fellow believers to pray for you that God may open a door for you to share the gospel with your unbelieving relatives, friends, and neighbors, as Paul did in Colossians 4:3–4: "[Pray] also for us, that God would open to us a door for the word, to speak the mystery of Christ, for which I am also in chains, that I may make it manifest, as I ought to speak." Ask them, too, to pray for you that God may not just open a door for you but open your mouth to speak boldly the message of the gospel. This was Paul's request from his fellow believers in Ephesus: "[Pray] for me, that utterance may be given to me, that I may open my mouth boldly to make known the mystery of the gospel, for which I am an ambassador in chains; that in it I may speak boldly, as I ought to speak" (Eph. 6:19–20).

Be honest with God about your fears in evangelizing. Are you afraid of being rejected? Jesus was rejected (John 1:11); thus, the experience of rejection is normal in evangelism. Are you afraid of offending your unbelieving relatives and neighbors? Well, expect them to be offended because the gospel is indeed offensive to the unbelievers (1 Pet. 2:7–8). Paul says, "For the message of the cross is foolishness to those who are perishing, but to us who are being saved it is the power of God" (1 Cor. 1:18).

Are you a shy or introverted person? Ask God to give you courage and zeal to share the glorious gospel with those who desperately need it (even in the form of a gospel tract). Pray along with the hymnwriter Herbert G. Tovey (1888–1972) to have a passion for the lost souls:

> Give me a passion for souls, dear Lord,
> A passion to save the lost;[4]
> O that Thy love were by all adored,
> And welcomed at any cost.
>
> Jesus, I long, I long to be winning
> Men who are lost, and constantly sinning;
> O may this hour be one of beginning
> The story of pardon to tell.
>
> How shall this passion for souls be mine?
> Lord, make Thou the answer clear;
> Help me to throw out the old Life-Line
> To those who are struggling near.[5]

---

4. This line echoes what Paul says in 1 Corinthians 9:22, "To the weak I became as weak, that I might win the weak. I have become all things to all men, that I might by all means save some."

5. Herbert G. Tovey, "A Passion for Souls," accessed November 14, 2023, https://hymnary.org/text/give_me_a_passion_for_souls_dear_lord.

In his book *Soul-Winner: How to Lead Sinners to the Saviour*, Charles Spurgeon expresses his similar passion to win souls for Christ. He insists that soul-winning, which he calls the "most royal employment," "should be the main pursuit of every true believer."[6] Interestingly, although Spurgeon understood well that ultimately only God can save or win souls, he did not hesitate to use the expression *soul-winning* to describe the work of evangelism. He argued that all believers "should each say with Simon Peter, 'I go a fishing,' and with Paul our aim should be, 'That I might by all means save some' [1 Cor. 9:22]."[7] In other words, in Spurgeon's mind, a soul-winner is much like a fisher of men.

In Matthew 4:19, Jesus calls Peter and Andrew and says to them, "Follow Me, and I will make you fishers of men." As Christ's followers, we are to fish sinners or win them for Christ by casting the net of the gospel over them, fully aware that only God can take them out of water or darkness of sin. In his work *The Art of Man-Fishing*, the Puritan pastor Thomas Boston (1676–1732) explains why the unconverted are compared to fish in the water. He says, "Among other reasons, they are so, because as the water is the natural element of fish, so sin is the proper and natural element of an unconverted soul. Take the fish out of the water, it cannot live; and take from a natural man his idols, he

---

6. Charles Spurgeon, *Soul-Winner: How to Lead Sinners to the Saviour* (New York/Chicago/Toronto: Fleming H. Revell Company, 1895), 7, 9.

7. Spurgeon, *Soul-Winner*, 9.

is ready to say with Micah. 'Ye have taken away my gods, and what have I more?'"[8] When was the last time you cast the gospel net over a fellow sinner? In case you have not yet done it, do it not only for others' sake but also for your own sake. You may not realize this, but evangelism is a spiritual discipline, and by spiritual discipline I mean a practice designed to deepen our relationship with God. Sadly, few Christians today view evangelism as a means by which they can grow in faith. When believers think of spiritual disciplines, they often think only of bible study, prayer, worship, fellowship, and others (excluding evangelism). In my own experience, evangelism helps me grow more in my understanding of the gospel I share with others. It also teaches me to become more dependent on God because I know unless He opens the spiritual eyes of the person I evangelize, this individual will not see the beauty and glory of Christ. Indeed, evangelism has many spiritual benefits for Christians. Therefore, I encourage you to participate in the work of evangelism for your own spiritual growth.

Also, as the Holy Spirit enables you, support an evangelistic cause. Before leaving for India, William Carey told his friends Andrew Fuller and Samuel Pearce, "I will go down into the pit, if you will hold the ropes."[9] Carey was aware of the difficulty of mov-

---

8. Thomas Boston, *The Art of Man-Fishing* (Glasgow, 1796), 9.

9. Cited in Nathan Finn, "Who Will Hold the Ropes: A Plea for Great Commission Pastors and Churches," accessed December 5, 2023, https://www.imb.org/2017/06/28/hold-ropes-plea-pastors-churches/.

ing to another country to serve as a missionary. He knew he could not be an effective missionary without others' help. He thus needed his fellow believers to hold the ropes for him as he descended into the pit of India (so to speak) to proclaim the gospel there. Thankfully, his friends held the ropes for Carey. They prayed for him, raised funds for him, and encouraged their own congregations to be involved in the mission work in India.

As I said earlier, while all of us are called to be ambassadors for Christ, not every one of us is called to leave his or her country and serve elsewhere as a missionary. Yet, these cross-cultural missionaries need their fellow believers back home to hold the ropes for them as they proclaim the gospel of Jesus Christ. You can hold the ropes in various ways—by encouraging missionaries, praying for them, and helping them with your financial resources. To inspire you in your own evangelistic endeavors, make time to read some good Christian books on the topic of evangelism and some good biographies of missionaries.

If you are a pastor or church leader, set a good example for your congregation. Don't expect your members to evangelize if you yourself do not evangelize. Our members usually learn by our example. Evangelism is an important aspect of your ministry. After Paul exhorted Timothy to "preach the word! Be ready in season and out of season," he reminds him not to neglect the work of evangelism: "But you be watchful in all things, endure afflictions, do the work of an evangelist, fulfill your ministry" (2 Tim. 4:5). To fully fulfill his ministry, Timothy must do his work as an evangelist. My fellow pastor, do you diligently perform your duty as an evangelist? I understand as a minister your primary calling is the two-fold ministry of prayer and of the word (Acts 6:4) — to pray for your congregation and "shepherd the flock of God which is among you" (1 Pet. 5:2). Yet, as Paul urges Timothy, do not neglect the work of evangelism. Pray evangelistically for the unconverted in your congregation and offer freely the gospel to them, calling them to faith and repentance. But think also of the unconverted in your community and neighborhood. Reach out to them as well with the gospel and be intentional in your evangelistic effort. Have you ever invited a neighbor to your house and to your church? If not, why not? Does it not bother you that even today you have not yet shared the gospel with anyone in your neighborhood? You're too busy? Is that a legitimate excuse? Remember the old saying, "Where there is a will, there is a way." Could it be the main reason you avoid evangelism is because you simply have no desire to do so?

In 1787, John Newton, best known today for his hymn "Amazing Grace," preached at the Annual Meeting of the Society for Promoting Religious Knowledge among the Poor. The title of his sermon was "The Best Wisdom," which was based on the second half of Proverbs 11:30 — "And he who wins souls is wise." In that sermon, while Newton acknowledged that "only [Jesus], who redeemed the soul by his blood, is able effectually to win [the soul] to himself,"

Newton declared how "the minister who winneth souls is wise." Then he added, "I trust, my brethren, we all desire to win souls."[10] My fellow ministers, do you desire to win souls or evangelize sinners?

And if you are a seminary professor, do not lose sight of the Great Commission. The seminary exists for the service of the church; and thus, you should regard your work as an extension of the ministry of the church. Whatever courses you teach—whether history, philosophy, or theology—should be intended for the growth of the church, "both in bringing in new members to it, and strengthening those that are brought in already."[11] Carl F. H. Henry (1913–2003) had the same concern when he said, "I don't think every seminary classroom should be turned into a course in evangelism, but there's something wrong if divinity professors consider their courses so irrelevant to fulfillment of the Great Commission that nowhere in the span of a year's teaching do students get any glimpse of personal concern for the lost."[12] Seminary teachers, do you help your students develop a love for the lost?

Now, brothers and sisters in the Lord, if you are too old or too weak to be actively engaged in evangelism, there are still ways in which you can be part of

---

10. John Newton, "The Best Wisdom" (1789), in *The Works of The Rev. John Newton*, vol. 9 (London, 1821), 179, 187.

11. Matthew Poole, *A Commentary on the Holy Bible*, vol. 3 (Peabody: Hendrickson, 1985), 672.

12. *Carl Henry at His Best: A Lifetime of Quotable Thoughts* (Portland: Multnomah Press, 1989), 73.

the work. You can pray. Learn to pray with the Scottish reformer John Knox, "Give me Scotland, or I die."[13] This earnest prayer shows Knox's intense desire for the conversion of Scotland. Paul voices a similar longing for Israel: "Brethren, my heart's desire and prayer to God for Israel is that they may be saved" (Rom. 10:1). Do you have the same desire and prayer to God for your fellow country people—that they might be saved? Pray with the English evangelist George Whitfield, "O Lord, give me souls or take my soul!"[14] Are you genuinely concerned with the salvation of your unconverted relatives and friends? Do you regularly pray for them? In addition to prayer, do you speak about God to your unbelieving family members and friends who come to visit you? If you are still able to speak coherently, you can also share the gospel with the caregivers who interact with you.

Finally, my fellow pastors and my fellow believers, live in such a way that you become a good witness for Christ in your family, church, school, workplace, and community (or wherever you are). Remember, you are "the salt of the earth" and "the light of the world" (Matt. 5:13–14). One of the uses of salt is to season food. As salt, then, you are to season the people around you with gospel flavor. That is, you are to influence them with your gospel living, marked by the fruit of the Spirit: "love, joy, peace, longsuffering, kindness,

---

13. Cited in Brian G. Najapfour, *The Collected Prayers of John Knox* (Grand Rapids: Reformation Heritage Books), xvii.

14. Cited in Zuck, *The Speaker's Quote Book*, 359.

goodness, faithfulness, gentleness, self-control" (Gal. 5:22–23). Salt is to be used; it should not remain in the cabinet; it should be put on the table for others to use. In a similar manner, you are not to be a closet Christian; don't hide your Christian identity. Let the people around you taste your gospel savor; let them know you are Christ's follower. Do the people you interact with daily know you are a Christian?

You are also called to shine as spiritual light in this sin-stricken, dark world. You are not to keep the gospel light to yourself. Let it be seen by others in your life. Let them be affected by its dazzling light, as Paul was in Acts 9:3. One hymnwriter articulates it this way:

> Send the light, the blessed gospel light;
> Let it shine from shore to shore!
> Send the light the blessed gospel light;
> Let it shine forevermore![15]

Or as Jesus says, "Let your light so shine before men, that they may see your good works and glorify your Father in heaven" (Matt. 5:16). Your life should reflect Jesus, who is ultimately "the light of the world" (John 8:12), the One who can dispel the darkness of sin. As the Puritan commentator Matthew Henry reiterates, "It is our duty not only to hold fast, but hold forth [the gospel called] the word of life; not only to hold it fast for our own benefit, but to hold it forth for the

---

15. Chas H. Gabriel, "There's a call comes ringing over the restless wave," accessed December 1, 2023, https://hymnary.org/text/theres_a_call_comes_ringing_oer_the_rest.

benefit of others, to hold it forth as the candlestick holds forth the candle."[16]

Be prepared, though, to face persecution as you faithfully let the gospel shine in your life, for it will inevitably provoke the wicked to hate you. Why? Because the gospel light will expose their evil deeds, and naturally the wicked don't want their evil deeds to be exposed. So we read in John 3:19–20: "the light [who is Jesus] has come into the world, and men loved darkness rather than light, because their deeds were evil. For everyone practicing evil hates the light and does not come to the light, lest his deeds should be exposed." Nevertheless, "Blessed are those who are persecuted for righteousness' sake," says Jesus, "for theirs is the kingdom of heaven" (Matt. 5:10). Therefore, keep shining before the world!

And despite persecution, be encouraged that no matter how Satan tries to stop the spread of the gospel, it will be spread triumphantly around the globe, for Jesus makes a promise that before He returns and judges the wicked, there will be a worldwide spread of the gospel. In His own words, "And this gospel of the kingdom will be preached in all the world as a witness to all the nations, and then the end will come" (Matt. 24:14). This does not mean though that all will be saved: some will receive the gospel, but others will reject it. Those who reject it will go away

---

16. Matthew Henry, *Commentary on the Whole Bible*, see his comments on Philippians 2:14–18.

into everlasting punishment, but those who believe will go into eternal life (25:46).

Let me end this book with an illustration that I heard several years ago. A little boy who had gone with his family to a family camp got lost in the forest. Though the family members and other people looked everywhere for him, they couldn't find him. After hours of searching, everyone returned to the camp, overwhelmed with disappointment. Then somebody suggested that they work their way back through the forest holding hands with one another, so as not to miss any area. They did this and soon found the boy, but it was too late. The boy was already dead. If only they had worked together in this way sooner, then—humanly speaking—they might have been able to save the boy's life.

My fellow believers in Christ, this is what we need to do as we seek to reach the lost who are perishing in their sins. I encourage you to spiritually hold the hand of your pastor, your elders, and your fellow church members. Let's hold hands together and proclaim the gospel of the Lord Jesus Christ in hopes that many who are dead in sin will soon be made alive in Christ by the power of the gospel (Eph. 2:4–5)!

APPENDIX ONE

Discussion Questions

Chapter 1: Introduction
1. Define evangelism in its broader sense.

2. Strictly speaking, is every Christian an evangelist? Explain your answer.

3. How does "the ministry of reconciliation" (2 Cor. 5:18) relate to the work of evangelism?

4. What is an ambassador for Christ (2 Cor. 5:20)? Is it basically the same as an evangelist?

5. Is the gospel only for unbelievers? If not, why?

6. In what sense do all Christians need to evangelize themselves?

7. How do Mark 1:15 and Acts 16:30–31 help us understand the gospel?

8. If an unbeliever were to ask, "What is the gospel?" what would you say? How can you explain the gospel to this individual?

9. Discuss John Owen's statement: "Gospel truth is the only root whereon gospel holiness will grow."

10. Discuss what is wrong about this statement addressed to William Carey: "Sit down, young man; when God wants to convert the heathen, He'll do it without your help or mine."

Chapter 2: Five Reasons Why All Christians Must Evangelize

1. How did the Christians in Acts 8:4 view evangelism? Is this how you also view evangelism?

2. Is evangelism a way of life for you? Is it part of your daily life? Do you evangelize regularly? If you do, share about one or two of your experiences.

Discussion Questions

3. Discuss this paragraph: "In Christ we are prophets and so we proclaim God's message, or in Christ we are evangelists and so we present the gospel. To put it another way, we proclaim Jesus because we are prophets, or we evangelize because we are evangelists. In short, evangelism is our identity in Christ."

4. Jesus commands us to love our neighbors as ourselves (Matt. 22:39). How can we best show to our unbelieving neighbors that we care for them?

5. Do your neighbors see and feel Christ's love in you? Do they even know you are a Christian? When was the last time you visited one of your neighbors and talked to him or her about the gospel?

6. What kind of effort do you make to build a bridge between you and your neighbors, so you can bring the gospel to them?

7. In what sense is God an evangelist? How did He evangelize you? When and how were you saved? If you don't know the exact date of your conversion, that is fine. But at least tell us the occasion or circumstance that God used for your

conversion. If God worked in your life as a young child, what fruits of God's saving grace have you seen in your life that assure you of your salvation? Or you may also want to share some of the changes in your life that you have noticed since you were saved.

8. Discuss this quotation by William Shedd: "It is the duty of the Christian Church to preach the gospel to every creature, because Christ the Head of the Church has commanded it so to do. It follows from this, that every individual member is obliged to contribute to this result, in proportion to his means and opportunity."

9. What should be our primary motivation in evangelism? Why should we evangelize?

10. Evangelism brings joy to the faithful Christian, but it also brings joy to the angels in heaven, and to our triune God whenever we do this! "I say to you," says Jesus, "there is joy in the presence of the angels of God over one sinner who repents" (Luke 15:10). When was the last time you experienced this kind of joy, the joy that flows out of the work of evangelism?

Chapter 3: Five Excuses Some Christians Use for Not Evangelizing

1. Discuss Moses's first excuse for not obeying God. How did God respond to Moses's excuse? What promise did God give to Moses to encourage him to go to Pharaoh to bring God's people out of Egypt?

2. How do you see yourself in Moses here? Perhaps you're saying something like this to God: "I am shy or an introvert." "I am weak." "I have no formal theological training." "I am afraid." And you're asking God, "Who am I that you would send me out to evangelize?"

3. Explain this statement: In evangelism, we are simply announcing the Good News — we are not teaching systematic theology or lecturing about church history or the five *solas* of the Reformation; and we are certainly not trying to discern for ourselves whether or not that person we evangelize is one of the elect of God.

4. What can we learn from Charles Spurgeon's experience when he simply stood before the seemingly empty room and cried in a loud voice, "Behold! The Lamb of God who takes away the sin of the world!" (John 1:29)?

5. What is the problem of hyper-Calvinism in evangelism?

6. How does the doctrine of election encourage us to evangelize?

7. In Exodus 4:10, Moses said to God, "I am not eloquent, neither before nor since You have spoken to Your servant; but I am slow of speech and slow of tongue." Why are these not legitimate excuses for not obeying God, or to apply it to evangelism, for not sharing the gospel with others?

8. What encouragement can we glean from Luke 12:11–12 and 1 Corinthians 2:1–4 as we do the work of evangelism?

9. Discuss this: We don't want to evangelize simply because we don't want to evangelize—and when we don't want to evangelize, we come up with alibis, or reasons that we shouldn't have to serve the Lord in this way.

10. Can you think of other excuses (not mentioned in the book) that Christians often use for not

evangelizing? How can you respond to these alibis from God's Word?

Chapter 4: Conclusion
1. Why do we all need the gospel?

2. Discuss: "To call the unbelievers to repent of their sins and believe in Christ may appear illogical. After all, unless God quickens dead souls, they cannot repent and believe, so it would seem to make more sense if God were to open their hearts to the gospel first, before we call them to repentance and faith. While this seems more logical to us, this is not the biblical pattern."

3. Do you ask your fellow believers to pray for you that God may open a door for you to share the gospel with your unbelieving relatives, friends, and neighbors?

4. Are you a shy or introverted person? If yes, do you ask God to give you courage and zeal to share the glorious gospel with those who desperately need it (even in the form of a gospel tract)? If no, then how are you boldly evangelizing?

5. Is the expression "soul-winning" biblical? Why?

6. How is evangelism a spiritual discipline? How can it help Christians deepen their faith in Christ?

7. Do you support missions? How? Do you pray for missionaries?

8. If you are a pastor, do you diligently fulfill your duty as an evangelist?

9. Why do we need to be prepared to face persecution as we faithfully let the gospel shine in our lives?

10. In Matthew 24:14, Jesus says, "And this gospel of the kingdom will be preached in all the world as a witness to all the nations, and then the end will come." How should this verse comfort us in evangelism?

APPENDIX TWO

Recommended Books on Evangelism

Beeke, Joel R. *Puritan Evangelism: A Biblical Approach.* Reformation Heritage Books, 2012.

Chantry, Walter J. *Today's Gospel: Authentic or Synthetic.* Banner of Truth Trust, 1970.

Denton, Ryan. *Even if None: Reclaiming Biblical Evangelism.* FirstLove Publications, 2019.

———. *Ten Modern Evangelism Myths: A Biblical Corrective.* Reformation Heritage Books, 2021.

Dever, Mark. *The Gospel & Personal Evangelism.* Crossway Books, 2007.

Kuiper, R. B. *God-Centered Evangelism.* Banner of Truth Trust, 1966.

MacArthur, John F. *Evangelism: How to Share the Gospel Faithfully.* Thomas Nelson, 2011.

Miller, C. John. *Powerful Evangelism for the Powerless.* P&R Publishing, 1997.

Packer, J. I. *Evangelism and the Sovereignty of God.* Intervarsity Press, 2012.

Phillips, Richard D. *Jesus the Evangelist: Learning to Share the Gospel from the Book of John*. Reformation Trust Publishing, 2007.

Reisinger, Ernest C. *Today's Evangelism: Its Message and Methods*. Craig Press, 1982.

Shedd, William G. T. "Every Christian a Debtor to the Pagans." In *Sermons to the Spiritual Man*, 385–99. Charles Scribner's Sons, 1884.

———. "The Certain Success of Evangelistic Labor." In *Sermons to the Spiritual Man*, 400–21.

Spurgeon, Charles H. *The Soul Winner*. Fleming H. Revell Company, 1895.

Tinker, Melvin. *Salt, Light and Cities on Hills: Evangelism, Social Action, and the Church: How Do They Relate to Each Other?* Evangelical Press, 2014.

APPENDIX THREE

A Gospel Tract:
Six Ways in Which Noah's Ark Is a Type of Christ[1]

Noah's ark is a type of Christ. It points us to some of the truths about the person and work of Jesus. How then is Noah's ark a type of Christ?

1. Just as the ark was graciously provided by God for sinners, so is salvation in Christ graciously provided by God for sinners (Gen. 6:13–14).

Noah by nature deserved to be destroyed because of his sin against God. "But Noah found favor [or grace] in the eyes of the LORD" (Gen. 6:8). God graciously provided him and his family the ark—a means through which they could escape from the flood of God's judgment against sin. Likewise, in our natural condition, we deserve to perish in hell; but God graciously provides us a savior in the person of His Son through whom we can escape from the fire of God's wrath in hell. Noah and his family did not deserve the ark. We do not deserve Christ, either. We do not

---

1. A version of this appendix originally appeared in *The Outlook* 67, no. 5 (2017): 17–18. Used with permission.

deserve heaven; we deserve hell. But God gives us the exact opposite of what we deserve: amazing grace!

2. Just as the ark was planned by God, so is salvation in Christ planned by God (Gen. 6:14–15).

Noah did not design the ark. God did. Noah did not plan for his deliverance. God did. In the same manner, God is the one who plans for our deliverance from the power and penalty of sin. God gives us His Son, so that through faith in Him we might be saved from sin. And God has planned this provision of salvation before the creation of the universe (Eph. 1:4). Imagine this: if you are a believer in Christ, God was already planning for your salvation even before you were born. He was already thinking of you, before you were even able to think of Him. You think of Him because He first thought of you.

3. Just as the ark was a place of safety, so is Christ a place of safety (Gen. 6:17).

The ark was a place of safety for Noah and his family. It sheltered them from the flood of God's judgment. Similarly, Jesus is our shelter against the storm of God's wrath. Those who are in Christ are protected, but those who are outside Christ are perishing. Indeed, those who are in Christ are saved forever. Those of you, however, who are struggling with assurance of salvation may say, "I believe in Jesus, but I don't feel like I am saved." Let me respond to you with this story:

A man once came to D. L. Moody and said he was worried because he didn't feel saved. Moody asked, "Was Noah safe in the ark?" "Certainly he was," the man replied. "Well, what made him safe, his feeling or the ark?" The inquirer got the point. "How foolish I've been!" he said. "It is not my feeling; it is Christ who saves!"[2]

4. Just as Noah and his family must come into the ark for their safety, so must we come to Christ for our salvation (Gen. 6:18).

God says to Noah, "You shall come into the ark—you, your sons, your wife, and your sons' wives with you" (Gen. 6:18). How shall they come into the ark?

First, *they shall come into the ark in response to God's command.* In Genesis 7:1, God commands Noah, "Come into the ark, you and all your household." To deliver them from the flood is God's work, but to enter the ark is their responsibility. If Noah and his family don't come into the ark, they will perish. Jesus also commands us to come to Him: "Come to Me... and I will give you rest" (Matt. 11:28). To give you rest is Christ's work, but to come to Him is your responsibility. You must come to Jesus by faith, or else your soul will forever be restless!

Second, *they shall come by faith in God's promise.* God's promise is twofold: to destroy those who don't believe in Him and to deliver those who believe in Him. Noah and his family believed God's promise,

---

2. Cited in Roy B. Zuck, *The Speaker's Quote Book* (Grand Rapids: Kregel, 1997), 18.

and so they entered the ark (Heb. 11:7). In the gospel, Jesus promises never to cast out those who come to Him (John 6:37). He promises to save those who believe in Him. Do you believe His promise?

Third, *they shall come into the ark individually*. Noah must enter the ark and so must his family. Noah cannot come on their behalf. They must come by themselves. In the context of salvation, no one can come to Christ on your behalf. You yourself must come to Jesus by faith. Salvation is personal.

5. Just as the call to come into the ark was a limited-time offer, so is God's call to come to His Son a limited-time offer (Gen. 7:16).

The door of the ark did not stay open indefinitely. God shut it in His appointed time for the protection of those inside and as a punishment for those outside.

Once the door has been shut, there is no more opportunity for people to come into the ark and be rescued from the flood of God's punishment. Oh, imagine those who were outside the ark when the flood came! "Seek the LORD while he may be found, call upon Him while He is near" (Isa. 55:6). Remember, the offer of the gospel is a limited-time offer. If you are still an unbeliever, I urge you to come to Jesus now for your salvation, while He may be found. Knock, while the door of heaven may be opened for you. Once the door is shut, there is no more hope for you. Oh, dear unbeliever, when will you repent of your sin and believe in the Lord Jesus Christ?

6. Just as the coming of the flood was unexpected, so is the second coming of Christ unexpected.
The flood came down suddenly upon the ungodly in Noah's day. Although they were informed and warned, they did not know the exact time of the coming of the flood.

Jesus proclaims, "But as the days of Noah were, so also will the coming of the Son of Man be. For as in the days before the flood, they were eating and drinking, marrying and giving in marriage, until the day that Noah entered the ark, and did not know until the flood came and took them all away, so also will the coming of the Son of Man be" (Matt. 24:37–39).

Jesus will come again, and He will come unexpectedly! Do you prepare for His return? Are you prepared to meet Him?

Concluding Thoughts

At Calvary, God poured His wrath upon His only begotten Son. The flood of God's wrath came upon His Son. God the Father shut the door of heaven, as it were, and Jesus was locked out. This inexpressible feeling of being shut out caused Jesus to cry out loudly, "My God, My God, why have You forsaken Me?" (Matt. 27:46). Imagine the cries of the people who were locked out in Noah's days. But here's the gospel: at Calvary, God locked His Son out, so that He could open the door of heaven for sinners who will believe in His Son. Through faith in Christ, sinners can now enter into the joy of heaven (Matt. 25:21). Do you believe in Jesus Christ? "He who believes in the Son has everlasting life; and he who does not believe the Son shall not see life, but the wrath of God abides on him" (John 3:36). Oh, by faith come to Jesus now!

ABOUT THE AUTHOR

Born and reared in the Philippines, Brian G. Najapfour holds a ThM from Puritan Reformed Theological Seminary in Michigan and a PhD from Theological University of Apeldoorn in the Netherlands. He has been a minister of the gospel since 2001 and has served both in the Philippines and in the U.S. He now lives in Canada, pastoring the Heritage Reformed Congregation of Jordan, Ontario. He has authored and coedited numerous books and has contributed several articles to journals, periodicals, and encyclopedias. He and his wife Sarah have five children. He enjoys exercising and playing basketball.

Other Books by the Author
Taking Hold of God: Reformed and Puritan Perspectives on Prayer. Coedited with Joel R. Beeke. Reformation Heritage Books, 2011.

The Very Heart of Prayer: Reclaiming John Bunyan's Spirituality. BorderStone Press, 2012.

Jonathan Edwards: His Doctrine of & Devotion to Prayer. Biblical Spirituality Press, 2013.

Child Dedication: Considered Historically, Theologically, and Pastorally. Biblical Spirituality Press, 2014.

Gospel-Driven Tongue: Lessons from James on Godly Conversation. Reformed Fellowship, Inc., 2017.

Amazing Grace. Co-authored with Sarah Najapfour. Biblical Spirituality Press, 2018.

The Collected Prayers of John Knox. Reformation Heritage Books, 2019.

A Hearer of God's Word: Ten Ways to Listen to Sermons Better. Reformed Fellowship, Inc., 2019.

Amazing Love! How Can It Be: Studies on Hymns by Charles Wesley. Coedited with Chris Fenner. Resource Publications, 2020.

www.ingramcontent.com/pod-product-compliance
Lightning Source LLC
Chambersburg PA
CBHW032047290426
44110CB00012B/987